United States Government Accountability Office

Report to Congressional Requesters

I0411704

July 2014

FEDERAL REAL PROPERTY

GSA Should Better Target Its Use of Swap-Construct Exchanges

July 2014

GAO Highlights

Highlights of GAO-14-586, a report to congressional requesters

FEDERAL REAL PROPERTY

GSA Should Better Target Its Use of Swap-Construct Exchanges

Why GAO Did This Study

To help address challenges in federal real-property management, including the growing need to replace and modernize federal buildings, GSA has proposed expanding its use of swap-construct exchanges. GSA has proposed this approach for some potentially large projects, including replacing the FBI's headquarters.

GAO was asked to review issues related to these exchanges. This report addresses: (1) GSA's experience with completed swap-construct exchanges; (2) the status of GSA's proposed swap-construct exchanges; and (3) the potential benefits of these exchanges and factors that can influence their future use. GAO reviewed documents, including GSA's solicitations for swap-construct exchanges, appraisals of completed exchanges, and OMB and GAO guidance. GAO conducted site visits to the completed swap-construct sites and three proposed swap-construct sites, selected based on location, number of responses to GSA's solicitation, and stage in the swap-construct process, and interviewed GSA officials and nonfederal participants in the exchanges.

What GAO Recommends

GAO recommends that GSA (1) include, to the extent possible, details on what GSA is seeking in exchange for federal property in these solicitations and (2) develop criteria for determining when to solicit market interest in swap-construct exchanges. GSA agreed with GAO's recommendations.

View GAO-14-586. For more information, contact Dave Wise at (202) 512-2834 or wised@gao.gov.

What GAO Found

Since 2000, the General Services Administration (GSA) has completed two "swap-construct" exchanges—transactions in which the agency exchanges title to federal property for constructed assets or construction services, such as renovation work—in response to private sector interest in specific federal properties. In both completed exchanges, GSA used the value of federal properties it determined were underutilized to acquire new parking garages. The recipients of the federal properties told us that the exchanges took longer than expected (about 3 years for one of the exchanges and 5 years for the other). In response, GSA noted its lack of experience with swap-construct exchanges at the time.

Since 2012, GSA has proposed six swap-construct exchanges. After reviewing responses to its solicitations, GSA is actively pursuing three, including a potential exchange of the existing Federal Bureau of Investigation's (FBI) headquarters for construction of a new FBI headquarters building. Respondents to the three solicitations that GSA is not actively pursuing noted concerns, including the amount of investment needed in the federal properties and the lack of detail regarding GSA's construction needs in an exchange. Swap-construct can result in an exchange of equally valued assets or services or can result in the government or a property recipient paying for a difference in value.

Proposed Swap-Construct Exchanges That GSA is No Longer Actively Pursuing

Spring Street Courthouse (Los Angeles, CA)   Metro West (Baltimore, MD)   Dyer Courthouse (Miami, FL)

Sources: GAO and GSA. | GAO-14-586

The swap-construct approach can help GSA address the challenges of disposing of unneeded property and modernizing or replacing federal buildings, but various factors could affect future use of the approach. For example, swap-construct can require developers to spend large sums on GSA's construction needs before receiving title to the federal property used in the exchanges. GSA's solicitations have not always specified these construction needs. Consequently, developers may be unable to provide meaningful input, and GSA could miss swap-construct opportunities. Further, the viability of swap-construct exchanges may be affected by specific market factors, such as the availability of alternative properties. However, GSA lacks criteria to help determine if the agency should solicit interest in a swap-construct exchange. As a result, GSA could miss opportunities to use swap-construct or select properties and construction projects better suited to traditional disposal and funding processes. Office of Management and Budget (OMB) and GAO guidance emphasize the importance of criteria in making capital-planning decisions and providing clarity on construction needs.

Contents

Abbreviations

ADA	Americans with Disabilities Act
FBF	Federal Buildings Fund
FBI	Federal Bureau of Investigation
GSA	General Services Administration
HEBSPC	H. E. Butt Store Property Company No. One
HEB	HEB Grocery Company
MARTA	Metropolitan Atlanta Rapid Transit Authority
OMB	Office of Management and Budget
RFI	request for information
RFP	request for proposals
RFQ	request for qualifications

July 24, 2014

Congressional Requesters:

The General Services Administration (GSA), which manages federal real property on behalf of other federal agencies, including real property acquisition, maintenance, and disposal, has faced long-standing challenges with underutilized properties and with securing funding for new construction and disposing of excess federal properties in a timely manner.[1] GSA also faces challenges replacing and maintaining aging federal properties due to the current fiscal environment of shrinking budgets throughout the federal government.[2] To help address these challenges, GSA has proposed expanding its use of "swap-construct" exchanges, whereby GSA receives either a constructed asset, such as a new building, or construction services, such as renovation work on an existing federal building, from a nonfederal entity in return for title to different federally owned property. GSA has proposed using swap-construct for several potentially large projects, including the consolidation of the Federal Bureau of Investigation's (FBI) headquarters operations into a new location, in exchange for the existing FBI headquarters building and its underlying land, and the relocation and consolidation of federal workers in the Federal Triangle South area of Washington, D.C., in exchange for federal buildings and their underlying lands.

Given the potential importance of swap-construct exchanges to addressing federal real property challenges, you asked us to review issues related these exchanges. This report addresses:

- GSA's experiences with completed swap-construct exchanges;

---

[1]We have previously found challenges with funding new construction, disposing of excess federal properties, and managing underutilized properties. See, GAO, *High-Risk Series: An Update*, GAO-13-283 (Washington, D.C.: February 2013); GAO, *Capital Financing: Alternative Approaches to Budgeting for Federal Real Property*, GAO-14-239 (Washington, D.C.: March 2014), and GAO, *Federal Real Property: The Government Faces Challenges to Disposing of Unneeded Buildings*, GAO-11-370T (Washington, D.C.: February 2011).

[2]Statement of the Honorable Daniel Tangherlini, Administrator for General Services Administration before the Subcommittee on Financial Services and General Government, Committee on Appropriations, House of Representatives (Apr. 8, 2014: Washington, D.C.).

- the status of GSA's proposed swap-construct exchanges; and
- the potential benefits of swap-construct exchanges and factors that can influence their future use.

To determine GSA's experience with swap-construct exchanges, we identified and reviewed the two completed swap-construct exchanges by reviewing GSA's exchange agreement documentation, appraisal reports, and related GSA guidance,[3] and interviewing GSA officials. To further understand these swap-construct exchanges, we conducted site visits to the locations of the exchanges (Atlanta, GA, and San Antonio, TX), examined the properties, and interviewed GSA and nonfederal participants in the exchanges. To determine the status of GSA's proposed swap-construct exchanges, we identified and reviewed the six exchanges proposed by GSA (two in Washington, D.C., and one each in Miami, FL; Los Angeles, CA; Baltimore, MD, and Lakewood, CO) using GSA documentation, including solicitations for market interest and ideas for addressing agency needs, called requests for information (RFI), and interviews with GSA officials. We visited three of the properties (two in Washington, D.C., and one in Baltimore, MD), which we selected based on proximity to GAO, number of RFI responses, and the stage at which the property was in GSA's swap-construct process. To understand GSA's authority to complete swap-construct exchanges, we reviewed relevant statutes and related GSA guidance. To further understand these proposed exchanges, we reviewed responses to the RFIs that GSA issued and conducted interviews with four of the seven respondents to two of the three proposed exchanges that GSA was no longer pursuing to further understand their experience with the proposals.[4] We selected the sample of respondents to include a variety of respondents, including a developer, a firm that advises developers, a university, and a company that provides property management services to the government.[5] To

---

[3] General Services Administration, *Guidance for Real Property Exchanges of Non-Excess Property* (Washington, D.C.: 1997).

[4] The two proposed exchanges from which we interviewed respondents were in Los Angeles, CA and Baltimore, MD. We did not conduct interviews with RFI respondents to the two proposed exchanges in Washington, D.C. since GSA is still actively in discussions or negotiations with these respondents.

[5] The views of these respondents cannot be generalized to make conclusions about all of the views of all respondents to GSA's proposed swap-construct exchanges. However, they illustrate the views of a diverse set of respondents with experience related to these exchanges.

understand the possible exchange in Lakewood, CO, we analyzed GSA documents, including agency property descriptions and tentative plans for the swap-construct exchange, and interviewed GSA officials and a local government official involved in the negotiations with GSA. To identify the potential benefits of swap-construct exchanges and factors that can influence their future use, we evaluated GSA's approach to identifying potentially successful swap-construct exchanges to propose for market interest against guidance from the Office of Management and Budget (OMB)[6] and GAO's Executive Guide on leading practices in capital decision-making,[7] and interviewed GSA officials, nonfederal participants in the two completed exchanges, affected stakeholders, and representatives of nongovernmental organizations familiar with GSA's real property projects. A full description of our scope and methodology can be found in appendix I.

We conducted this performance audit from September 2013 to July 2014 in accordance with generally accepted government auditing standards. Those standards require that we plan and perform the audit to obtain sufficient, appropriate evidence to provide a reasonable basis for our findings and conclusions based on our audit objectives. We believe that the evidence obtained provides a reasonable basis for our findings and conclusions based on our audit objectives.

Background

GSA follows a prescribed process for the disposal of federal properties that are reported as excess by federal agencies[8]—a process that can take years to complete. GSA first offers excess property to other federal agencies. If no federal agency needs it or homeless provider expresses an interest in it, the property becomes surplus and may be made available for other uses through a public benefit conveyance, when state and local governments, and certain nonprofits, can obtain the property at

---

[6]Office of Management and Budget, *Supplement to Circular No. A-11: Capital Programming Guide* (Washington, D.C.: July 2012).

[7]GAO, *Executive Guide: Leading Practices in Capital Decision-Making,* GAO/AIMD-99-32 (Washington, D.C., December 1998). GAO identified leading practices by interviewing and reviewing documentation from government and private sector organizations identified through consultation with experts in the fields of capital planning and decision-making.

[8]According to GSA, if a federal agency no longer needs property it is considered excess property.

up to 100 discount of fair market value when it is used for public purposes, such as an educational facility. Ultimately, the property may be disposed of by a negotiated sale for public use or public sale based on GSA's determination of the property's highest and best use.

GSA collects rent from tenant agencies, which is deposited in the Federal Buildings Fund (FBF) and serves as GSA's primary source of funding for operating and capital costs associated with federal real property. Congress exercises control over the FBF through the appropriations process, which designates how much of the fund can be obligated for new construction and maintenance each fiscal year.[9] According to GSA, capital funding has not kept pace with GSA's need to replace and modernize buildings in its federal real property portfolio, which includes about 1,500 buildings. We have recently found that GSA and other federal agencies have pursued alternative approaches to address challenges with funding federal real property projects.[10] One alternative approach is a swap-construct exchange between the federal government and a nonfederal entity, such as a private developer. GSA has several authorities to exchange federal property for constructed assets and, in 2005, was specifically authorized to exchange federal property for construction services.[11]

Swap-construct exchanges can be proposed by a nonfederal entity, such as a private developer or local government, or by GSA. GSA's process for proposing and conducting a swap-construct exchange includes either proposing a swap-construct exchange to a nonfederal entity that has expressed an interest in acquiring a specific federal property or soliciting market interest through an initial proposal, often an RFI, followed by more detailed proposals. These more detailed proposals include requests for qualifications (RFQ) to identify qualified developers and requests for proposals (RFP). In a swap-construct exchange, the federal government transfers the title of the federal property to a developer or other property recipient after receiving a constructed asset or the completion of

---

[9]GAO has previously reported on the Federal Buildings Fund. See GAO, *Federal Buildings Fund: Improved Transparency and Long-term Plan Needed to Clarify Capital Funding Priorities*, GAO-12-646 (Washington, D.C.: August 2012).

[10]GAO-14-239.

[11]See 40 U.S.C. § 3304(a); 40 U.S.C. § 3305(a)(1); 40 U.S.C. § 3305(a)(2); 40 U.S.C. § 581(c)(1); 40 U.S.C. § 543; and Pub. L. No. 108-447, § 412 (Dec. 8, 2004).

construction services at a different location. Swap-construct exchanges can involve swapping property and constructed assets or construction services that are of equal value or can include cash to compensate for a difference in value between the federal property and the asset or services to be received by the government. According to GSA, highest priority is assigned to swap-construct exchanges that involve exchanges of federal property of equal or greater value than the asset or services provided by the property recipient because these scenarios do not require appropriation of federal funding. Figure 1 describes GSA's decision-making process for proposing swap-construct exchanges and the three scenarios that can result from an agreement for a swap-construct exchange.

Figure 1: GSA's Decision Making Process for Swap-Construct Exchanges and Three Exchange Scenarios

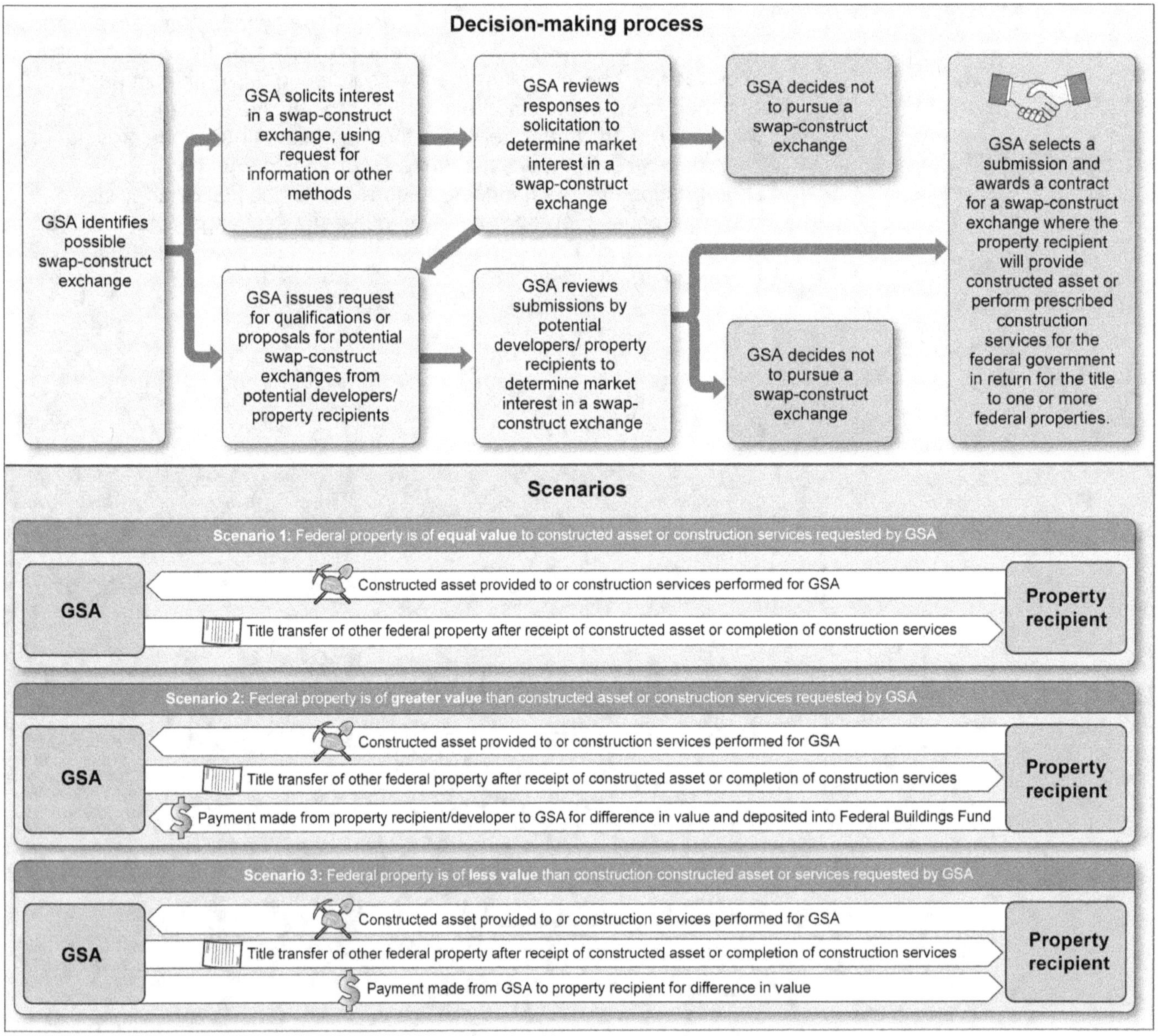

Decision-making process

GSA identifies possible swap-construct exchange

→ GSA solicits interest in a swap-construct exchange, using request for information or other methods

→ GSA reviews responses to solicitation to determine market interest in a swap-construct exchange

→ GSA decides not to pursue a swap-construct exchange

GSA issues request for qualifications or proposals for potential swap-construct exchanges from potential developers/ property recipients

→ GSA reviews submissions by potential developers/ property recipients to determine market interest in a swap-construct exchange

→ GSA decides not to pursue a swap-construct exchange

→ GSA selects a submission and awards a contract for a swap-construct exchange where the property recipient will provide constructed asset or perform prescribed construction services for the federal government in return for the title to one or more federal properties.

Scenarios

Scenario 1: Federal property is of **equal value** to constructed asset or construction services requested by GSA

GSA — Constructed asset provided to or construction services performed for GSA → Property recipient

Title transfer of other federal property after receipt of constructed asset or completion of construction services

Scenario 2: Federal property is of **greater value** than constructed asset or construction services requested by GSA

GSA — Constructed asset provided to or construction services performed for GSA → Property recipient

Title transfer of other federal property after receipt of constructed asset or completion of construction services

$ Payment made from property recipient/developer to GSA for difference in value and deposited into Federal Buildings Fund

Scenario 3: Federal property is of **less value** than construction constructed asset or services requested by GSA

GSA — Constructed asset provided to or construction services performed for GSA → Property recipient

Title transfer of other federal property after receipt of constructed asset or completion of construction services

$ Payment made from GSA to property recipient for difference in value

Source: GAO analysis of GSA information. | GAO-14-586

According to GSA, once the agency has decided to pursue an exchange for a newly constructed asset or services, it follows GSA's 1997 guidance for real property exchanges of non-excess property.[12] The guidance lays out a number of steps, including:

- obtaining a property appraisal;
- using, if possible, one appraiser for all properties involved in an exchange; and
- analysis and documentation of all benefits and costs of the exchange to show why the exchange is in the best interest of the government.

In November 2013, the GSA Inspector General issued a memo noting that GSA's 1997 guidance is not specifically applicable to exchanges of real property for services.[13] In responding to the memo, GSA stated that it was in the process of preparing guidance specific to exchanges for services.

GSA's Experience with Swap-Construct Is Limited to Two Exchanges for Parking Garages That Were Initiated by Private Sector

Since 2000, GSA has completed two swap-construct exchanges initiated by companies—Emory University Hospital Midtown (then called Emory Crawford Long Hospital) and H. E. Butt Store Property Company No. One (HEBSPC)—that were interested in acquiring specific federal properties in Atlanta, GA and San Antonio, TX, respectively. A now-retired representative of Emory University Hospital Midtown and representatives of HEBSPC told us that they were satisfied with the end result of the exchanges, but added that there were challenges in the process that may affect future swap-construct exchanges. Specifically, the representatives told us that the exchanges took longer than anticipated, about 3 years in Atlanta and over 5 years in San Antonio, and that, consequently, less motivated parties may avoid or withdraw from future exchanges. GSA officials told us that both exchanges were a good value for the government because the properties and services received by the government were of equal or greater value than the federal properties disposed of in the exchanges. GSA officials added that the exchanges

---

[12]General Services Administration, *Guidance for Real Property Exchanges of Non-Excess Property* (Washington, D.C.: 1997). As previously discussed, properties declared excess follow a prescribed disposal process.

[13]General Services Administration, Office of Inspector General, *PBS Needs to Develop Policies and Procedures for Use of Section 412 Authorities*, Audit Memorandum A130132 (Washington, D.C.: November 2013).

were a good value for the government because both of the assets disposed of were underutilized. However, these officials noted their lack of experience with swap-construct exchanges at the time.

Atlanta Swap-Construct—In 2001, GSA exchanged a federal parking garage (the Summit Garage) in Atlanta with 1,829 spaces on a 1.53-acre parcel with Emory University Hospital Midtown for a newly constructed parking garage (the Pine Street Garage) with 1,150 spaces on .92 acres (see fig. 2). GSA also received a commitment from the hospital to lease and manage the operations and maintenance of the Pine Street Garage for 16 years and to lease spaces in it to federal employees. According to GSA, at the time of the exchange, the Summit Garage was underutilized because it included more parking spaces than GSA needed.[14] Although GSA utilized some of the extra spaces through a lease agreement with the hospital, which is located nearby, the garage was, GSA added, in deteriorating condition and was not it compliance with the Americans with Disabilities Act (ADA). According to GSA, the swap-construct exchange was in the best interest of the government because GSA received a new ADA-compliant garage with a direct covered connection to both the Peachtree Summit Federal building and a Metropolitan Atlanta Rapid Transit Authority (MARTA) subway station in exchange for a garage that was underutilized and in deteriorating condition. GSA added that the exchange was beneficial to the government because it included the hospital's commitment to lease spaces not needed by the government for 16 years, with proceeds deposited into the FBF, and to cover operations and maintenance work typically covered by GSA.[15]

[14]The Summit building and garage were built for a private sector company and later acquired by the federal government. The Summit Garage was originally intended to accommodate two office towers, only one of which, the current Peachtree Summit Federal Building, was constructed.

[15]According to GSA, at the end of lease, GSA can extend the lease with the hospital or issue another solicitation for prospective bidders.

GAO-14-586 Federal Real Property

Figure 2: Map and Images of Parking Garage Disposed (top) and Parking Garage Received (bottom) by GSA in Atlanta Swap-Construct Exchange

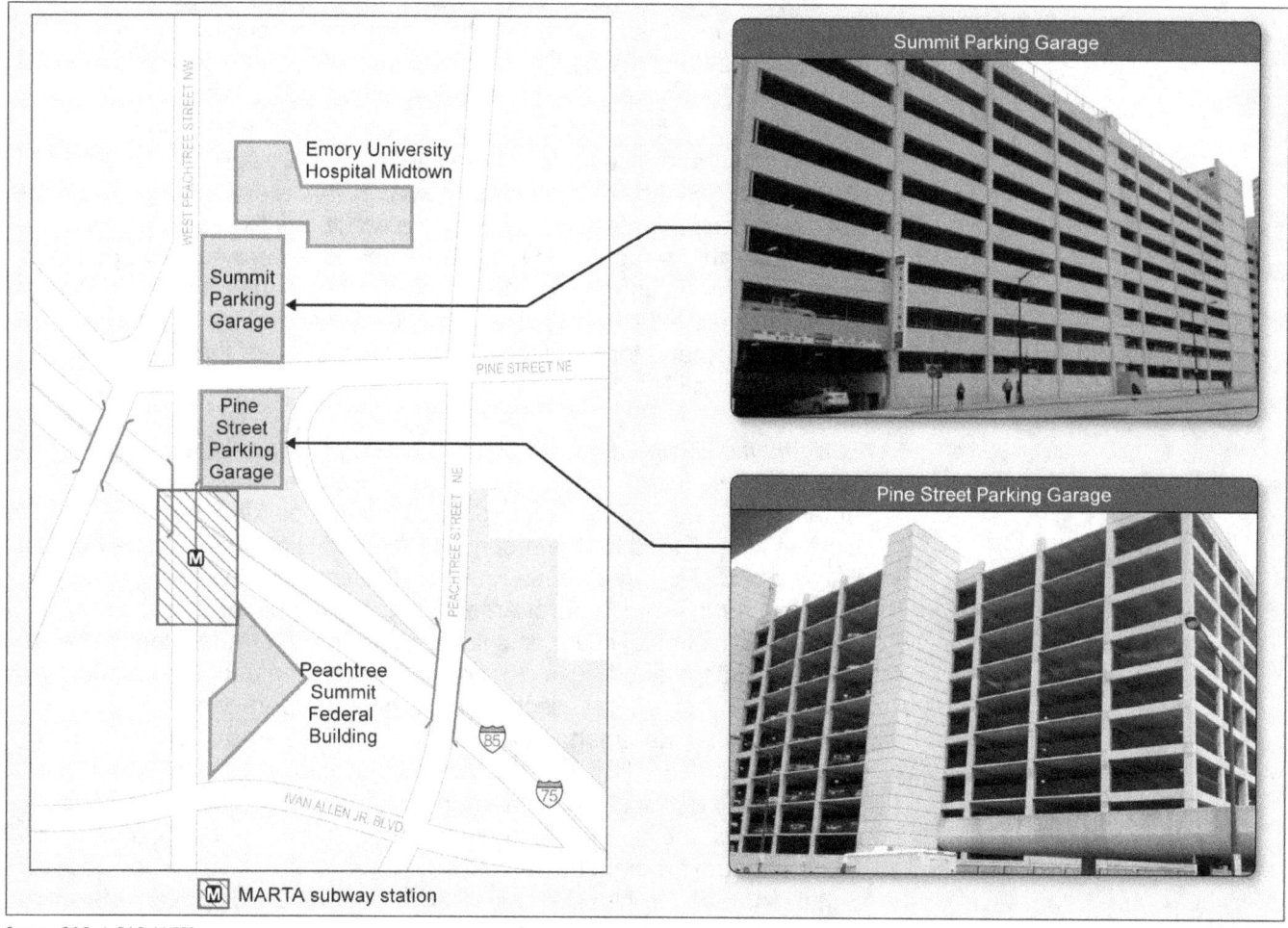

Source: GAO. | GAO-14-586

According to the now-retired representative of Emory University Hospital Midtown who was involved with the swap-construct exchange, the acquisition of the Summit Garage was crucial to accommodating a hospital renovation and expansion project. However, the hospital was aware that GSA needed parking spaces to accommodate federal tenants in the Peachtree Summit Federal Building, so it proposed the swap-construct approach to GSA. The representative added that, although the hospital was pleased with the end result of the transaction, the exchange took about 3 years to complete, a time that was longer than anticipated for the hospital and that may lead less motivated parties to avoid or withdraw from future exchanges. GSA officials noted that the agency had limited experience with this type of exchange, which may have contributed to the length of time required to complete it. The representative added that the exchange was also complicated in that the appraised value of the new garage and any additional services had to be equal to the appraised value of the Summit Garage.[16] The now-retired representative added that to address concern that the new and smaller garage might appraise for less than the Summit Garage, the hospital agreed with GSA to continue leasing spaces in the new garage and cover operations and maintenance costs. As a result, the two parts of the exchange—the garages and lease agreements—were equally appraised at $6.6 million. According to GSA, although the hospital's lease in the new garage expires in 2017, the size of the garage allows the agency to meet continued demand for federal parking in the vicinity of the Peachtree Summit Federal Building.

San Antonio Swap-Construct—In 2012, GSA exchanged an approximately 5-acre federal property (the Federal Arsenal site) in San Antonio, TX, with HEBSPC for construction of a parking garage on existing federal land for the recently renovated Hipolito F. Garcia Federal Building and U.S. Courthouse (see fig. 3). According to GSA, at the time of the exchange, the Federal Arsenal site was an underutilized asset because of historical covenants limiting the ability to redevelop the land and its buildings and because it was located on the periphery of the city away from other federal assets. Although the property was partly utilized by GSA's Fleet Management and through a lease agreement with HEB Grocery Company (HEB)[17] for parking spaces, GSA officials told us that there was no anticipated long-term government need for it. According to GSA officials, the swap-construct exchange was in the best interests of the federal government because the government received a new federal parking garage for the Hipolito F. Garcia Federal Building and U.S. Courthouse in exchange for a property that was underutilized.

---

[16]According to GSA officials, GSA's policy goal is for the government to receive equal or better than fair market value for swap-construct exchanges.

[17]According to an HEBSPC representative, HEB is a retail grocery store with whom HEBSPC engages in business transactions. The two companies are separate and neither is a subsidiary of the other.

GAO-14-586 Federal Real Property

Figure 3: Map and Images of Parking Garage Received (top) and Federal Property Disposed (bottom) by GSA in San Antonio Swap-Construct Exchange

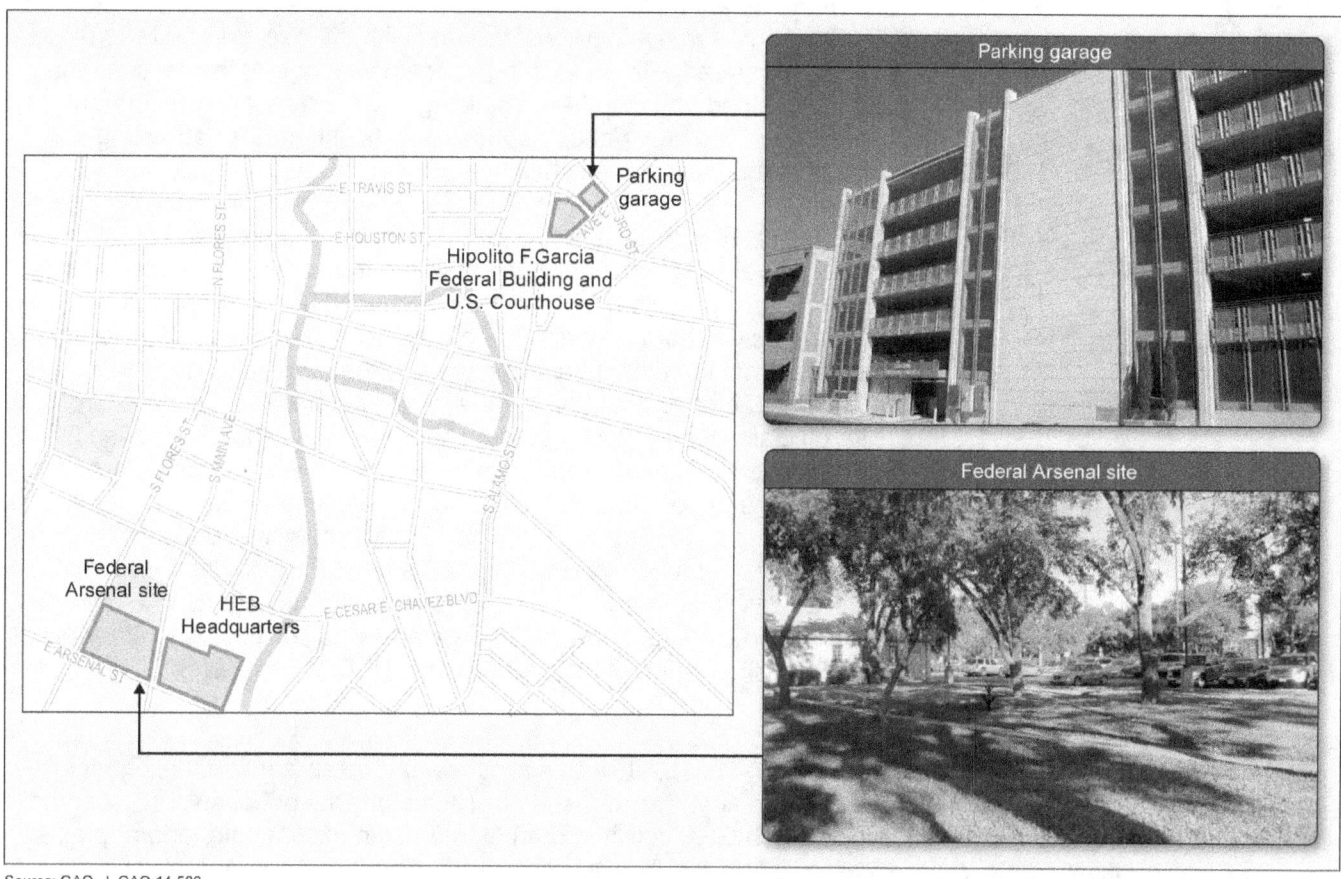

HEBSPC representatives told us that the company was interested in acquiring the Federal Arsenal site to accommodate existing space needs and potential expansion of HEB's corporate headquarters, near the site and expressed this interest to GSA. The representatives added that although the historic covenants on the property presented some potential challenges, the company had prior experience renovating and utilizing historic properties on HEB's headquarters property. The representatives also told us that the company had a long-standing interest in acquiring the Federal Arsenal site prior to 2005, but during that time, the property could not be sold because it was being partly used by GSA's Fleet Management. In 2005, however, GSA told HEBSPC about the need for an additional parking for the Hipolito Garcia Federal Building and U.S.

Courthouse and, subsequently, proposed the swap-construct exchange to HEBSPC, which had experience building parking garages. An official from one of the tenant agencies in the federal building and courthouse told us that the increased availability of parking with the new garage (150 new spaces compared with 35 existing spaces) was one of the reasons the agency decided to locate in the building. GSA officials told us that the availability of the new parking spaces is critical to further attracting tenants to the building, which is not fully occupied.

HEBSPC representatives told us the company was pleased with the transaction and GSA's management of the transaction. However, they added that they would have preferred it to have been completed quicker than the 5-plus years between the proposal and exchange of properties, and noted that the time it took to complete the transaction may lead less motivated parties to avoid or withdraw from such exchanges. According to GSA officials, the transaction took longer than anticipated because GSA did not have significant experience to use as a basis for completing the transaction and because of fluctuations in real estate values due to the economic recession that required additional property appraisals to be completed. After four property appraisals between 2007 and 2009, GSA and HEBSPC ultimately valued the Federal Arsenal site at $5.6 million. According to GSA, the new parking garage was constructed to fully utilize the $5.6 million value of the property that HEBSPC received.

GSA Is Pursuing Half of Its Six Swap-Construct Proposals

Since August 2012, GSA has proposed six swap-construct exchanges— one that the agency proposed directly to the City of Lakewood, CO, and five in which GSA solicited market interest in exchanging federal property, totaling almost 8-million square feet, for construction services or newly constructed assets. After reviewing responses to these six proposals, GSA is actively pursuing three, including: (1) a potential exchange of undeveloped federal land in Denver with the City of Lakewood for construction services at the Denver Federal Center; (2) a potential exchange of the existing FBI headquarters building for a new FBI headquarters building; and (3) a potential exchange of two federal buildings in the Federal Triangle South area of Washington, D.C., for construction services to accommodate federal workers elsewhere in the city. According to GSA officials, although the agency has had authority to exchange property for construction services since fiscal year 2005 and had authority to exchange property for newly constructed assets prior to that, until recently there has been limited agency interest using non-traditional property disposal and acquisition approaches, such as swap-construct exchanges. The officials added that since 2012 the agency has more widely pursued swap-construct exchanges to address challenges such as a rising number of agency needs and limited budgetary resources. According to GSA officials, although the projects could involve exchanges of equal value, similar to the Atlanta and San Antonio exchanges, they could result in the government either receiving a payment or paying to cover any difference in value between the property to be exchanged and its construction projects.

GSA decided to propose a swap-construct exchange to the City of Lakewood because the city had previously expressed interest in the undeveloped federal land, totaling about 60 acres, and because GSA had need for construction services at the nearby Denver Federal Center. A representative of the City of Lakewood told us that the city was supportive of the swap-construct approach because the services provided to GSA would support employment for the local population, whereas if the city were to purchase the property through a sale, the proceeds would not necessarily be spent locally. GSA told us that negotiations for a possible swap-construct exchange are ongoing.

We found that respondents expressed openness or interest in the swap-construct approach regarding four of the five exchanges for which GSA solicited market interest, but generally this openness or interest was limited to the proposed consolidation of the FBI's headquarters operations into a new location in exchange for the existing FBI headquarters building and land. Several responses to GSA's RFIs did not address swap-construct and instead provided other information, such as the credentials of a particular developer and statements that GSA should ensure that affordable housing is included in the redevelopment of federal properties to be exchanged. Figure 4 describes swap-construct exchanges for which GSA solicited market interest and responses to its RFIs.

Figure 4: Swap-Construct Exchanges for Which GSA Solicited Market Interest, 2012–2013

Federal Triangle South properties (Washington, DC)

Cotton Annex	GSA Regional Office Building	U.S. Department of Energy Forrestal Building	Federal Aviation Administration (FAA) Orville Wright Building	FAA Wilbur Wright Building

• Built 1937 • Eligible for the National Register of Historic Places • About 100,000 sq. ft. • 1.7 acres of land	• Built 1932 • About 900,000 sq. ft. • 3 acres of land	• Built 1968 • About 1.8 million sq. ft. • 15.9 acres of land	• Built 1963 • About 1 million sq. ft. • 3.6 acres of land	• Built 1964 • Eligible for the National Register of Historic Places • About 420,000 sq. ft. • 2.2 acres of land

Request for Information (RFI) date: December 3, 2012[a]

GSA's stated need in RFI for exchange involving the federal properties: Construction of office space to meet the long-term needs of federal employees currently housed in aging and inefficient properties in the Federal Triangle South properties. Construction services to address long-term space needs of other federal employees in the Washington, D.C. area will also be considered.

10 RFI responses: 2 respondents open to or supportive of a swap-construct exchange.

J. Edgar Hoover Building (Washington, DC)	Spring Street Courthouse (Los Angeles, CA)	Metro West (Baltimore, MD)	Dyer Courthouse (Miami, FL)

• Built 1971 • Headquarters of Federal Bureau of Investigations • About 2 million sq. ft. • 6.7 acres of land	• Built 1940 • Listed on the National Register of Historic Places • About 800,000 sq. ft. • 3.7 acres of land	• Built 1980 • About 1 million sq. ft. • 11 acres of land	• Built 1933 • Listed on National Register of Historic Places • About 180,000 sq. ft. • 1.6 acres of land
RFI date: January 9, 2013	**RFI date:** December 10, 2012	**RFI date:** August 8, 2013	**RFI date:** August 1, 2012
GSA's stated need in RFI for exchange involving the federal property: Construction services to consolidate FBI headquarters staff into a new building.	**GSA's stated need in RFI for exchange involving the federal property:** A new federal building at a separate federal property.	**GSA's stated need in RFI for exchange involving the federal property:** Construction services at other, unspecified, GSA-held properties.	**Construction priorities requested by GSA:** Unspecified construction service related to redevelopment of Dyer Courthouse.
38 RFI responses: 21 respondents open to or supportive of a swap-construct exchange.	**4 RFI responses:** 3 respondents open to or supportive of a swap-construct exchange.	**3 RFI responses:** 1 respondent open to or supportive of a swap-construct exchange.	**2 RFI responses:** No interest in swap-construct exchange.

Sources: GAO and GSA. | GAO-14-586

[a]An RFI is a solicitation for market interest and ideas in addressing an agency's needs.

For the proposed FBI headquarters swap-construct exchange, GSA officials told us that the agency anticipates identifying qualified developers by fall 2014 and awarding a contract to a developer for the transaction in summer 2015. For the proposed swap-construct exchange involving Federal Triangle South properties, GSA narrowed the scope of its proposed exchange after reviewing responses to its RFI. Specifically, in April 2014, the agency issued an RFQ to identify qualified developers for a potential exchange involving two of the five properties included in the RFI—the Cotton Annex and the GSA Regional Office Building—for renovations to GSA's headquarters building and construction services to support the Department of Homeland Security's headquarters consolidation in Washington, D.C.

GSA officials told us that there was little or no market interest in potential swap-construct exchanges in Baltimore, MD (the Metro West building) and Miami, FL (the David W. Dyer Courthouse[18]), and that different approaches were now being considered to address them. In addition, although GSA received some interest in a swap-construct exchange involving another property, the U.S. Courthouse at 312 N. Spring Street in Los Angeles (hereafter referred to as "the Spring Street Courthouse"), GSA officials said the agency may need to pursue other approaches for this property as well. The respondents to these potential exchanges expressed various concerns. For example, 4 of 9 respondents expressed concerns about the lack of detail regarding what GSA would expect in return for the federal property and 4 of 9 respondents expressed concerns about the amount of investment needed in the federal properties to make the exchange profitable for the property's recipient. Three RFI respondents and representatives of one nongovernmental organization familiar with GSA's real property projects added that swap-construct may be a less viable approach in markets with a large number of alternative real estate options.

According to developers and organizations familiar with GSA's swap-construct proposals, the two exchanges for which GSA solicited market interest and is still pursuing generally benefit from the inclusion of federal properties located in an area with high real-estate values and, thus, profitable redevelopment potential. Specifically, both properties are

---

[18]A swap-construct exchange was one of several options listed in GSA's RFI for the David W. Dyer Courthouse. These options included an exchange, exchange for services, lease, or sale of the property.

located in areas of Washington, D.C., near mass transit and prominent landmarks (see fig. 5). In addition, one of the potential projects—the consolidation of the FBI headquarters operations into a new location—benefits from a well defined scope with GSA's expectations for the construction priority being sought by the agency in exchange for the federal property considered for exchange in the proposal—the J. Edgar Hoover Building. In 2011, GSA estimated that a new FBI headquarters built on federal land would cost about $1.9 billion.[19] According to GSA, this estimate is out of date.

---

[19]According to GSA, this figure represents the cost of initial development and long-term ownership, including recurring operations, maintenance, and repair expenses over a 30-year period, discounted to 2011.

Figure 5: Location of Properties Being Considered for Exchange by Swap-Construct in Washington, D.C.

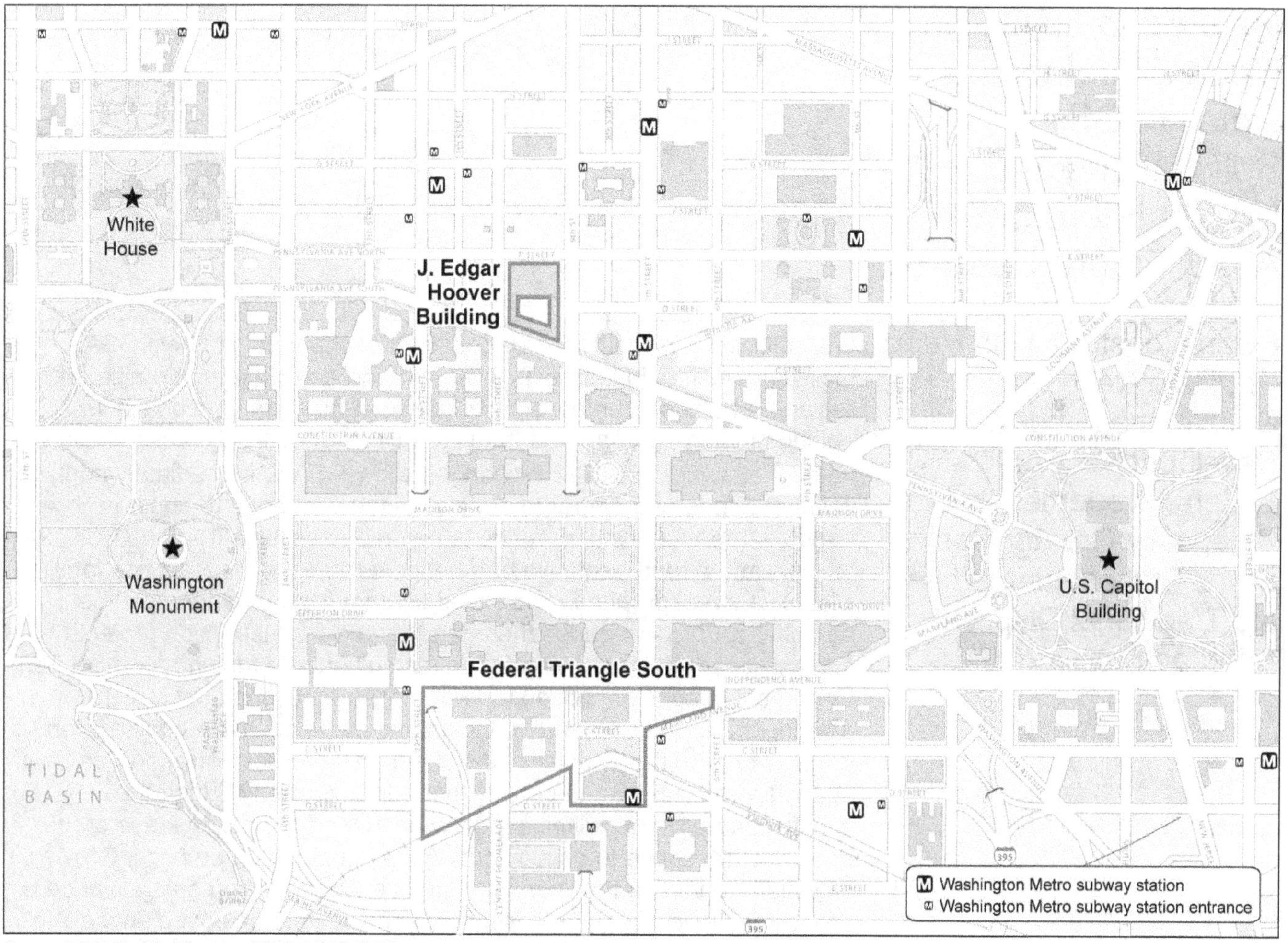

Sources: U.S. National Park Service and GAO. | GAO-14-586

Swap-Construct Can Help Address GSA's Needs, but Level of Detail in GSA's Solicitations and Market Interest May Affect Future Use

Swap-Construct Can Help Facilitate New Construction and Developer Access to Federal Properties, but at Potentially Greater Cost to Some Stakeholders Than the Traditional Disposal Approach

GSA officials told us that swap-construct exchanges can help GSA facilitate construction projects given a growing need to modernize and replace federal properties, shrinking federal budgets, and challenges getting funding appropriated from the FBF.[20] Specifically, GSA officials noted that swap-construct exchanges allow GSA to immediately apply the value of a federal property to be used in the exchange to construction needs, rather than wait for funds to be made available from the FBF. GSA officials and a representative of a nongovernmental organization familiar with GSA's real property projects added that the exchanges can be attractive for GSA because the agency can get construction projects accomplished without having to request full upfront funding for them from Congress. In addition, because swap-construct exchanges require developers or other property recipients to address GSA's construction projects prior to the transfer of the title to the exchange property, federal agencies can continue to occupy the federal property during the construction process, eliminating the need for agencies to lease or acquire other space to occupy during the construction process. GSA officials also told us that swap-construct exchanges can help advance a government-wide goal to consolidate agencies out of leased space into federally owned space. For example, according to GSA, about half of the FBI's headquarters staff are located in the existing headquarters building and the potential swap-construct exchange for a new FBI headquarters could allow the agency to consolidate into one federally owned building.

---

[20]We have previously reported that, historically, the FBF has been challenged to provide sufficient revenue to support GSA's real property portfolio. In recent years, budgeting and appropriations decisions made by the executive branch and Congress, respectively, have limited the amount of resources made available to GSA to fund its real property operations. See GAO-12-646 and GAO-14-239.

The retired Emory University Hospital Midtown representative and HEBSPC representatives added that swap-construct exchanges can help the private sector acquire federal property that it otherwise may not be able to acquire.

While swap-construct can facilitate GSA's construction needs, it could come at a greater cost to some stakeholders than the traditional disposal approach. Specifically, because federal properties disposed of through swap-construct are not declared excess or surplus (often because they are still in use by federal tenants when the swap-construct is proposed and during the exchange process), they do not go through the traditional disposal process. Thus, the swap-construct approach may limit the participation of nonfederal entities that would have been interested in acquiring the properties through public benefit conveyance or other means. For example, in a typical property disposal, eligible public and nonprofit entities, such as institutions of higher education or homeless organizations, can receive the federal property at up to a 100 percent discount of fair market value when it is used for a variety of qualified purposes, such as education and assistance for the homeless. Two institutions of higher education that responded to GSA's solicitations for a swap-construct exchange expressed a preference for GSA to use the traditional disposal process because the universities could then obtain it by public benefit conveyance. A representative of a national advocacy group for the homeless expressed concern that swap-construct could serve as a way around the traditional disposal process and believes GSA should offer public benefit conveyances prior to proposing swap-construct exchanges.

GSA Does Not Always Clearly Identify Its Needs in Its Solicitations for Market Interest in Swap-Construct Exchanges

Swap-construct exchanges require developers to make potentially large investments in federal construction projects prior to receiving title to federal property used in the exchanges. GSA's solicitations for market interest in swap-construct projects do not always clearly identify what projects the agency is seeking in exchange for the federal property. For example, the RFIs for the potential Dyer Courthouse and Metro West swap-construct exchanges did not specify what GSA was seeking as part of an exchange. Two respondents to the Metro West RFI told us that additional details regarding what GSA expects in return for the property would be key to future consideration of a swap-construct exchange. In addition, one developer we spoke to told us that the lack of detail regarding what GSA expected in return for the Metro West property influenced his company's decision not to respond to the RFI. One of the four respondents to the Spring Street Courthouse RFI added that although GSA specified a need for a new building in exchange for the Spring Street Courthouse, it was not clear that the new building was a GSA priority. Specifically, the respondent noted that future swap-construct exchanges may benefit from additional information on GSA's needs, such as a strategic plan for a region where GSA is proposing a swap-construct exchange.

GSA officials also told us that the agency does not always identify its needs prior to releasing its RFIs for swap-construct exchanges. OMB guidance notes that although federal agencies should not specify requirements too narrowly in RFIs, agencies should identify clear agency needs in the documents.[21] Leading practices also note the importance of identifying an agency's needs[22] and being transparent about these needs.[23] GSA officials acknowledged that while details were not always specified in RFIs for swap-construct exchanges, details would be specified in subsequent solicitations if GSA determines there is enough market interest based on the RFI responses. GSA officials also stated that fewer details were included in the RFIs because the agency wanted to gauge market interest in the swap-construct transaction structure and did not want to limit the creativity of potential RFI respondents. However, by not providing some detail on the agency's needs in its RFIs, GSA risks limiting respondents' ability to provide meaningful input and could miss potential swap-construct opportunities for the properties.

Various Factors May Affect the Applicability of Swap-Construct Exchanges, and GSA Lacks Criteria for Identifying Good Exchange Candidates

GSA has generated interest in swap-construct for some projects, as previously discussed, but several factors may limit the applicability of the agency's approach. Three of the four RFI respondents and one of the two nongovernmental organizations we spoke to noted that the federal property to be exchanged should have high redevelopment potential to offset the developers' risk of delayed access to the property until providing GSA with its needed asset or construction services. Specifically, a developer may have to expend significant time and money addressing GSA's needs for a new building or renovating an existing federal building before receiving, redeveloping, and generating revenue from the

---

[21]OMB, *Capital Programming Guide.*

[22]GAO/AIMD-99-32.

[23]GAO 12-646.

swapped federal property. GSA officials told us that it might be possible to negotiate some early rights of access to the federal property before the transfer of the property title to conduct activities such as site preparation and demolition work, but at a developer's risk. According to representatives of the two nongovernmental organizations we spoke to, GSA should also consider local market conditions in deciding if a property is suitable for swap-construct because developers can often purchase or lease similar properties they need from the private sector and quickly access them for redevelopment. For example, a representative of a firm that advises developers noted that the FBI headquarters building is located in an area of Washington, D.C., with high potential for profitable redevelopment and that there are few other similar properties available to developers. In contrast, a Metro West RFI respondent and a Spring Street Courthouse RFI respondent expressed concern that the federal properties included in those exchanges, in Baltimore and Los Angeles, respectively, may not have sufficient redevelopment potential to offset the risks associated with delayed transfer of title under a swap-construct approach.

Potential complications with exchanging property in one region for a constructed asset or construction services in another region may also limit the applicability of swap-construct exchanges. Specifically, GSA officials told us that the pool of potential bidders is smaller and community and political opposition can be higher when removing federal assets from one region for a constructed asset or construction services in another. In addition, the officials said project management can be more difficult for GSA when an exchange is executed across different regions. Consequently, the officials told us they try to locate the desired constructed asset or construction services in the same region as the federal property to be exchanged. GSA officials added that many underutilized federal properties are not suitable for swap-construct because they are in locations where GSA has limited needs for new assets or construction services or because the federal properties are not sufficiently desirable or would require too much investment from a developer.

A representative of the firm that advises developers added that while the swap-construct approach gives GSA greater control over the proceeds from a property disposal, the federal government may get a better deal for a new asset or construction services and potentially larger proceeds for the disposed federal property if it were to use traditional acquisition and disposal methods. In particular, the representative noted that developers may be willing to pay more for federal property through a sale because the developers could gain immediate access to the property for redevelopment purposes. Similarly, the representative told us that GSA may get a better deal on a new asset or construction services it if were to pursue them through a traditional acquisition process because it would invite more developer competition into the process, unlike in a swap-construct approach where a developer would also need to be willing to receive federal property as consideration.

While GSA has guidance for determining if it should continue to pursue an exchange that has already been proposed, it does not have criteria to help determine when the agency should solicit interest in a swap-construct exchange. According to GSA officials, the agency considers possible swap-construct exchanges on a case-by-case basis during its annual review of its entire federal real property portfolio, but it lacks guidance on how that case-by-case analysis should be conducted. GSA officials added that because the agency only recently started using the swap-construct approach, it does not have screening criteria for determining when a swap-construct exchange should be proposed. Moreover, we found that some proposed swap-construct exchanges have been driven by GSA's need to dispose of specific federal properties and that, as previously discussed, GSA has not given the same amount of consideration to construction projects to include in its proposed exchanges. For example, in the Metro West and Dyer Courthouse swap-construct proposals, GSA identified federal properties to be exchanged, but little or no information on construction projects it needed in a potential exchange.

GSA has proposed swap-construct exchanges since 2012 to a mixed reception, as previously noted, with little or no interest in exchanges involving the Dyer Courthouse in Miami, the Spring Street Courthouse in Los Angeles, and the Metro West building Baltimore, and high level interest in an exchange only for the FBI headquarters consolidation project. Both OMB and GAO guidance emphasize the importance of using criteria to make capital-planning decisions.[24] By not using screening criteria to identify potentially successful swap-construct exchanges, the agency may miss the best opportunities to leverage swap-construct

---

[24]OMB, *Capital Programming Guide, Supplement to Office of Management and Budget Circular A-11: Planning, Budgeting, and Acquisition of Capital Assets* (Washington, D.C.: July 2013), and GAO, *Executive Guide: Leading Practices in Capital Decision-Making*, GAO/AIMD-99-32 (Washington, D.C.: December 1998).

exchange or select properties for exchange that are better suited to the traditional property disposal process and construction projects that are better suited to traditional funding processes. GSA may also waste time and money pursuing a potential swap-construct exchange that could be better spent pursuing these traditional approaches.

Conclusions

GSA faces some key challenges in managing its federal real property portfolio, especially in disposing of unneeded federal property and financing the replacement or modernization of aging and underutilized properties. In some cases, the swap-construct approach discussed in this report might be a useful means through which GSA can more readily achieve these property-related goals. However, GSA's recent solicitations for market interest in swap-construct have not always been well received by potential bidders. Specifically, of the five swap-construct exchanges GSA for which GSA solicited market interest since 2012, only two are being actively pursued; the others generated little market interest. One concern for potential bidders was the lack of detail regarding the construction services that GSA hoped to gain in return for an asset it would cede to the bidder. We found that in developing initial proposals for a swap-construct exchange GSA often focused on identifying assets to dispose of and gave less attention to what it needed in exchange for those assets. Construction services or a newly constructed asset are fully half of any swap-construct exchange, yet GSA has not always clearly identified its needs when requesting feedback from potential bidders. The agency's intent may be to provide greater details at later stages of the proposal process, but this approach may limit the ability of respondents to provide meaningful input and lead to missed swap-construct opportunities for GSA.

At present GSA does not have criteria for identifying viable exchanges in the sense that both sides of the potential transaction are fully defined and communicated to potential interested parties. OMB and GAO have previously identified the importance of criteria in making agency decisions. By not using screening criteria to make its choices, GSA may be pursuing swap-construct exchanges with less potential for success, and potentially delaying time that it could be spending on traditional disposal and appropriation processes. Similarly, GSA may also miss opportunities to leverage swap-construct more widely moving forward, which could be crucial given ongoing budgetary challenges.

Recommendations

In order to identify potentially successful swap-construct exchanges during GSA's review of its federal real property portfolio and reduce uncertainty for those responding to GSA's solicitations for possible swap-construct exchanges, we recommend that the Administrator of GSA take the following two actions:

1. include, to the extent possible, details on what GSA is seeking in exchange for federal property in its solicitations, including requests for information, for potential swap-construct exchanges and

2. develop criteria for determining when to solicit market interest in a swap-construct exchange.

Agency Comments

We provided a draft of this report for review and comment to GSA. GSA concurred with the report's recommendations and provided additional information on the proposed swap-construct exchange with the City of Lakewood, Colorado, which we incorporated. GSA's letter is reprinted in appendix II.

As arranged with your offices, unless you publicly disclose the contents earlier, we plan no further distribution of this report until 30 days after the date of this letter. At that time, we will send copies of the report to the Administrator of GSA. Additional copies will be sent to interested congressional committees. We will also make copies available to others upon request, and the report is available at no charge on the GAO website at http://www.gao.gov.

If you have any questions about this report, please contact me at (202) 512-2834 or wised@gao.gov. Contact points for our Offices of Congressional Relations and Public Affairs may be found on the last page of this report. Major contributors to this report are listed in appendix III.

David J. Wise
Director
Physical Infrastructure Issues

List of Congressional Requesters

The Honorable Thomas R. Carper
Chairman
The Honorable Tom Coburn, M.D.
Ranking Member
Committee on Homeland Security and Governmental Affairs
United States Senate

The Honorable Darrell Issa
Chairman
The Honorable Elijah E. Cummings
Ranking Member
Committee on Oversight and Government Reform
House of Representatives

The Honorable John L. Mica
Chairman
Subcommittee on Government Operations,
Committee on Oversight and Government Reform
House of Representatives

Appendix I: Objectives, Scope, and Methodology

Our objectives were to determine (1) GSA's experiences with completed swap-construct exchanges; (2) the status of GSA's proposed swap-construct exchanges; and (3) the potential benefits of swap-construct exchanges and the factors that can influence their future use. We described GSA's swap-construct process using information gathered from GSA guidance[1] and interviews with GSA officials. In addition, we reviewed related laws that facilitate GSA's swap-construct exchanges.[2]

To determine GSA's experience with swap-construct exchanges, we identified and reviewed the two swap-construct exchanges (Atlanta, GA, and San Antonio, TX) completed by GSA since 2000 through GSA exchange agreement documentation, appraisal reports, and property descriptions, and through interviews with GSA officials. We conducted site visits to Atlanta and San Antonio, examined the properties involved in the exchanges, and interviewed GSA officials and nonfederal participants—H. E. Butt Store Property Company No. One (HEBSPC) and Emory University Hospital Midtown—about their experience with the transactions.

To determine the status of GSA's proposed swap-construct exchanges, we identified and reviewed the six proposed swap–construct exchanges—two in Washington, D.C., and one each in Miami, FL; Los Angeles, CA; Baltimore, MD; and Lakewood, CO—using GSA documentation, including GSA solicitations for possible exchanges, known as requests for information (RFI), and through interviews with GSA officials. We conducted site visits to three of the properties involved in the proposed exchanges (the Cotton Annex and Regional Office Building in Washington, D.C and the Metro West building in Baltimore, MD), examined the properties, and spoke with GSA officials about the RFIs that included these properties. We selected these properties based on nearby proximity (within a 50-mile radius) and to include a site visit to both a location where the property or properties in the RFI generated 10 or more responses and to a location were the property or properties in the RFI generated fewer than 10 responses. To further identify a property or

---

[1]General Services Administration, *Guidance for Real Property Exchanges of Non-Excess Property* (Washington, D.C.: 1997).

[2]40 U.S.C. § 3304(a); 40 U.S.C. § 3305(a)(1); 40 U.S.C. § 3305(a)(2); 40 U.S.C. § 581(c)(1); 40 U.S.C. § 543; and Pub. L. No. 108-447, § 412.

properties to visit, we then limited our selection to property or properties
that were furthest along in GSA's proposed swap-construct process. In
addition, to better understand the status of these proposed exchanges,
we analyzed the responses GSA received to its solicitations for these
swap-construct exchanges and discussed the proposed exchanges with
four of the seven respondents to the Metro West and Spring Street
Courthouse RFIs. We did not interview RFI respondents to the proposed
swap-construct exchanges that involved the FBI headquarters and
Federal Triangle South properties since GSA is actively in discussions or
negotiations with these respondents. We selected our sample of the
respondents to include a variety of respondents, including a development
company, firm that advises developers, a university, and a company that
provides property management services to the government. Because the
RFI respondents were selected as a nonprobability sample, the
information gained in these interviews cannot be generalized to make
conclusions about all of GSA's swap-construct exchanges. However, they
illustrate the views of a diverse set of respondents with experience related
to these exchanges. To understand the possible exchange in Lakewood,
CO, we analyzed GSA documents, including agency property
descriptions and tentative plans for the swap-construct exchange, and
interviewed GSA officials and a local government official involved with the
negotiations with GSA.

To identify the potential benefits of swap-construct exchanges and factors
that can influence GSA's future use these exchanges, we evaluated
GSA's approach to identifying potentially successful swap-construct
exchanges to propose against the OMB *Capital Programming Guide*[3] and
the GAO *Executive Guide on Leading Practices in Capital Decision-
Making*,[4] and interviewed GSA officials; nonfederal participants in
completed swap-construct exchanges (HEBSPC and Emory University
Hospital Midtown); stakeholders in federal property acquisition and
disposal processes (the National Capital Planning Commission and the
National Law Center for Homelessness and Poverty, respectively); and
nongovernmental organizations familiar with GSA's swap-construct
exchanges (the National Council for Public-Private Partnerships and the

---

[3]OMB, *Supplement to Circular No. A-11: Capital Programming Guide* (Washington, D.C.:
July 2012).

[4]GAO, *Executive Guide: Leading Practices in Capital Decision-Making,* GAO/AIMD-99-32
(Washington, D.C., December 1998).

Urban Land Institute). In addition, we analyzed written responses GSA received to its solicitations for proposed swap-constructs exchanges and information from interviews we conducted with the four respondents, described above, to identify any factors that may affect GSA's future use of swap-construct exchanges.

We conducted this performance audit from September 2013 to July 2014 in accordance with generally accepted government auditing standards. Those standards require that we plan and perform the audit to obtain sufficient, appropriate evidence to provide a reasonable basis for our findings and conclusions based on our audit objectives. We believe that the evidence obtained provides a reasonable basis for our findings and conclusions based on our audit objectives.

Appendix II: Comments from the General Services Administration

The Administrator

July 3, 2014

The Honorable Gene L. Dodaro
Comptroller General of the United States
U.S. Government Accountability Office
Washington, DC 20548

Dear Mr. Dodaro:

The U.S. General Services Administration (GSA) appreciates the opportunity to review and comment on the draft report entitled *Federal Real Property: GSA Should Better Target Its Use of Swap-Construct Exchanges* (GAO-14-586).

As the Government's real estate expert, GSA is considering new approaches to real property asset management that leverage the value of properties in the Public Buildings Service portfolio. By exchanging these properties with public or private entities that will derive greater value from them, GSA can acquire services to address critical infrastructure needs in its owned portfolio. As noted in the U.S. Government Accountability Office (GAO) report, these swap-construct opportunities enable GSA to reposition portfolio assets in a manner that facilitates the modernization or replacement of buildings within its aging portfolio, as well as take advantage of consolidation and space reduction opportunities.

To that end, GAO recommends that the GSA Administrator:

> (1) Include, to the extent possible, details on what GSA is seeking in exchange for Federal real property in its solicitations, including requests for information, for potential swap construct exchanges; and

> (2) Develop criteria for determining when to solicit market interest in a swap-construct exchange.

GSA agrees with the first recommendation.

To the extent that GSA has specific details available regarding the services or property it will seek in exchange for the subject real property, those details are included in the Request for Information (RFI). It is in GSA's interest that an RFI be as detailed as

U.S. General Services Administration
1800 F Street, NW
Washington, DC 20405
Telephone: (202) 501-0800
Fax: (202) 219-1243

2

possible so that the best possible market information can be collected. However, in some instances, GSA uses the RFI to assess the feasibility of a swap-construct exchange as a viable strategy, and defining the required outcome too narrowly or prescriptively might constrain options presented by potential offerors. As GSA continues to refine its best practices regarding swap-construct exchanges, GSA will include detailed information in Requests for Qualifications, Requests for Proposals or other similar forms of solicitation, and will include detailed information in RFIs, whenever possible.

GSA also agrees with the second recommendation and has developed criteria for determining when to solicit market interest in a swap-construct exchange. This criteria has been included in agency-wide guidance, which GSA recently provided to GAO. In addition, substantive technical comments updating and clarifying statements in the draft report are enclosed.

If you have any additional questions or concerns, please do not hesitate to contact me at (202) 501-0800, or Ms. Lisa Austin, Associate Administrator, Office of Congressional and Intergovernmental Affairs, at (202) 208-1806.

Sincerely,

Dan Tangherlini
Administrator

Enclosure

cc: Phillip Herr, Director, Physical Infrastructure Issues

Appendix III: GAO Contact and Staff Acknowledgments

GAO Contact

Dave J. Wise at (202) 512-2834 or at wised@gao.gov

Staff Acknowledgments

In addition to the contact named above, Keith Cunningham, Assistant Director; Amy Abramowitz; Dawn Bidne; Timothy Guinane; James Leonard; Sara Ann Moessbauer; Josh Ormond; and Crystal Wesco made key contributions to this report.

Related GAO Products

Capital Financing: Alternative Approaches to Budgeting for Federal Real Property. GAO-14-239. Washington, D.C.: March 12, 2014.

Federal Real Property: Excess and Underutilized Property Is an Ongoing Challenge. GAO-13-573T. Washington, D.C.: April 25, 2013.

High-Risk Series: An Update. GAO-13-283. Washington, D.C.: February 14, 2013.

Federal Courthouses: Recommended Construction Projects Should Be Evaluated under New Capital-Planning Process. GAO-13-263. Washington, D.C.: April 11, 2013.

Federal Buildings Fund: Improved Transparency and Long-term Plan Needed to Clarify Capital Funding Priorities. GAO-12-646. Washington, D.C.: July 12, 2012.

Federal Real Property: National Strategy and Better Data Needed to Improve Management of Excess and Underutilized Property. GAO-12-645. Washington, D.C.: June 20, 2012.

Federal Real Property: The Government Faces Challenges to Disposing of Unneeded Buildings. GAO-11-370T. Washington, D.C.: February 10, 2011.

Federal Courthouse Construction: Estimated Costs to House the L.A. District Court Have Tripled and There Is No Consensus on How to Proceed. GAO-08-889. Washington, D.C.: September 12, 2008.

Federal Real Property: Most Public Benefit Conveyances Used as Intended, but Opportunities Exist to Enhance Federal Oversight. GAO-06-511. Washington, D.C.: June 21, 2006.

Executive Guide: Leading Practices in Capital Decision-Making. GAO/AIMD 99-32. Washington, D.C.: December 1, 1998.

GAO's Mission	The Government Accountability Office, the audit, evaluation, and investigative arm of Congress, exists to support Congress in meeting its constitutional responsibilities and to help improve the performance and accountability of the federal government for the American people. GAO examines the use of public funds; evaluates federal programs and policies; and provides analyses, recommendations, and other assistance to help Congress make informed oversight, policy, and funding decisions. GAO's commitment to good government is reflected in its core values of accountability, integrity, and reliability.
Obtaining Copies of GAO Reports and Testimony	The fastest and easiest way to obtain copies of GAO documents at no cost is through GAO's website (http://www.gao.gov). Each weekday afternoon, GAO posts on its website newly released reports, testimony, and correspondence. To have GAO e-mail you a list of newly posted products, go to http://www.gao.gov and select "E-mail Updates."
Order by Phone	The price of each GAO publication reflects GAO's actual cost of production and distribution and depends on the number of pages in the publication and whether the publication is printed in color or black and white. Pricing and ordering information is posted on GAO's website, http://www.gao.gov/ordering.htm. Place orders by calling (202) 512-6000, toll free (866) 801-7077, or TDD (202) 512-2537. Orders may be paid for using American Express, Discover Card, MasterCard, Visa, check, or money order. Call for additional information.
Connect with GAO	Connect with GAO on Facebook, Flickr, Twitter, and YouTube. Subscribe to our RSS Feeds or E-mail Updates. Listen to our Podcasts. Visit GAO on the web at www.gao.gov.
To Report Fraud, Waste, and Abuse in Federal Programs	Contact: Website: http://www.gao.gov/fraudnet/fraudnet.htm E-mail: fraudnet@gao.gov Automated answering system: (800) 424-5454 or (202) 512-7470
Congressional Relations	Katherine Siggerud, Managing Director, siggerudk@gao.gov, (202) 512-4400, U.S. Government Accountability Office, 441 G Street NW, Room 7125, Washington, DC 20548
Public Affairs	Chuck Young, Managing Director, youngc1@gao.gov, (202) 512-4800 U.S. Government Accountability Office, 441 G Street NW, Room 7149 Washington, DC 20548